Table of Contents

* Full color transparencies are found at the back of the book. Each
transparency should be used to introduce the corresponding unit.

Teaching Guide

This book has been designed to strengthen map reading and
analyzing skills and to familiarize students with the features of
different regions of the United States. Each section contains a
student page and an accompanying map that is used to complete the student page. Each page builds upon previous pages
and students should have access to all previously completed
maps. Encourage students to use latitude and longitude mark-
ings when comparing features between maps. Students may
use related resources to assist them in completing the student
pages. Accept all reasonable answers that can be logically
supported. Color transparencies, located in the back of the
book, will assist you in your classroom presentation.

Map 1: The United States in the World

This Robinson projection map provides a continuous map
with relatively little distortion of shapes and sizes. It is a
compromise between rectangular projections such as the
Mercator or Peters and more accurate interrupted projections.

The student page offers directional activities and a world overview.

Extension Activities:

1. Have students locate the origins of products found in the classroom such as clothing and personal items. Trace the trade routes that bring materials and products from other lands to the United States.

2. Use this map to discuss the European exploration of the world. Have students trace the routes of Ericson, Columbus, Dias, Da Gama, and Magellan.

3. Use this map to plot civilizations in existence in 1000 A.D. and compare with concurrent Native American civilizations. Color the boundaries of Native American civilizations.

4. Trace shipping routes that took settlers and materials to California during the gold rush. Compare these routes with the overland route.

Map 2: North America

This map should build familiarity with the continental setting of the United States and may be used for a variety of teaching opportunities. The student page offers practice in map reading and latitude/longitude skills.

Extension Activities:

1. Have students write stories about an imaginary early explorer of the new world.

2. Trace routes of European explorers. Include all of the voyages of Columbus but do not neglect the other explorers. You may wish to use separate maps to show the various routes of explorers during a specific time frame.

3. Plot Native American civilizations on the map. Compare and contrast Native American lifestyles as they are affected by region.

4. Trace the spread of early Native Americans over the continent beginning with the Bering Land Bridge.

Map 3: States and Capitals

This map can be used for latitude and longitude practice or the map can be labelled using a classroom atlas or textbook.

Extension Activities:

1. Make a copy of the map. Using different colors for specified date ranges, have students color the states according to when statehood was achieved.

2. Make choropleth maps to study a variety of statistics. A choropleth map uses a different color for a different range. Example: have students research the average incomes or high school graduation rates and create their own maps displaying this information.

3. Make a map showing the spread of women's suffrage through the various states. Color code the map.

Map 4: Physical Features

The student page provides a narrative description of the features of the United States and students will label the features on the map. Alternatively, the teacher may wish to number the features on the map and then have students match these with the feature names. The map has not been numbered

to provide maximum flexibility.

Extension Activities:

1. Have students draw the borders of the continental plates. This information can be found in most encyclopedias and atlases.

2. Have students use an atlas to find the latitudes and longitudes of several high peaks and locate them on their maps.

3. Research routes of early land explorers and/or trade routes and trace them on this map. Have students write travel logs of early explorers describing land features they would have seen.

4. Have students separate land and water features and label two different copies of the map.

5. Students may make three-dimensional maps with clay or papier-mâché. Alternatively, they can put layers of cardboard cut to correct dimensions for different elevations. For example: use one layer for every 500 ft. or 100 meters of elevation.

6. Students may use this map as a base for creating a land use map. Land use information may be found in an encyclopedia or textbook.

7. Use this map as a base for creating a vegetation map. This map can then be compared to the climate and precipitation maps.

Map 5: Climate and Precipitation

Introduce or review climate types with the students. Point out that different classification systems are used by geographers and that the one given is a simplified system. The precipitation map provides opportunities to discuss the effects of landforms and ocean currents on continental precipitation. For example: Study the effect of the Sierra Nevada and Cascades on precipitation in the Great Basin. The student page provides practice in locating geographic areas, comparing maps, and learning about climates.

Extension Activities:

1. Use an almanac to find exact precipitation records for cities in the United States. Construct bar or line graphs to compare cities in different areas.

2. Students may write about climates and their effect on outdoor activities and life-styles.

3. Compare the effect of climate and precipitation on land use activities.

Map 6: Expansion of the American Republic

This map documents the growth of the United States throughout history. The student page provides a narrative description of this growth, basic questions on the material, and labeling and coloring activities. This map could be used throughout a course of study, coloring the areas as the events unfold or it can be used with the student page as a review.

Extension Activities:

1. Research the areas in the different divisions. Find out how many square miles are in each one. Arrange this information in a bar or circle graph.

2. Using the same data as above, prepare a line graph showing the areal growth of the United States.

3. Trace routes that led to the opening of the west: Lewis and Clark, Fremont, Oregon Trail, Santa Fe Trail, Pony Express, Union Pacific Railroad, etc.

Map 7: Origins of State Names
The student page gives interesting information on the origins of state names.

Extension Activities:
1. Gather information on the origins of major river names and compare the patterns with those of the states.

2. Repeat this activity with city or county names in your state.

3. This base map can be used to create a products map. Students may gather necessary information from a textbook or encyclopedia.

4. This map can also be used to color the separate nations that existed during the American Civil War. Different colors should be used to designate the North, the South, border states, and territories.

Map 8: Population Density and Large Cities
The term *density* refers to the average number of people per square mile or kilometer. Parts of the United States are densely populated while others are nearly barren. Areas that are not densely populated are probably low in arable land, high in elevation, or far north. On the other hand, areas which in most countries would be unpopulated support a large population in the U.S. (e.g. southern Arizona). The relative wealth and technological level of the U.S. makes this possible. Teachers should discuss the reasons for the variance of population considering climate, precipitation, physiography, and political borders. Teachers should also discuss the geographic advantages of different cities and their effect on population. The student page offers practice in labeling, map reading, and interpretation.

Extension Activities:
1. Assign students to research different states. Have them research other maps and/or encyclopedias and write a paragraph explaining reasons for existing population patterns.

2. Consult an almanac to determine the present population of large cities. Add to the map any cities that have grown to more than one million people.

3. Consult an almanac and compare population densities of the U.S. with those of other countries; also compare birthrates and life expectancies.

4. Students may work in groups to determine factors that have led to the growth of different cities.

Map 9: Transportation
These maps provide basic information on major transportation routes throughout the United States. The student page provides practice in locating geographic areas, river names, and states.

Extension Activities:
1. Students can plan their own trips.

2. Using encyclopedia articles on the states, students can show how producers move goods from sources to markets and which means are best.

3. Students can create quiz questions to be used in class: "What is the city where these two interstates meet?" etc.

Maps 10-16: Regional Maps
These maps provide details for map study or for regional study of the United States. The student pages provide labeling activities for improving mental mapping, latitude and longitude practice, direction and scale practice, and comparative geography. Only major features and cities are shown and teachers may wish to add more. Teachers may also wish to make two copies of each map for students: one for use with physical features and one for working with cities.

Extension Activities:
1. Color the maps to make the state borders more obvious and to make the map more aesthetically pleasing.

2. Make overlays showing climates, elevations, or precipitation levels.

3. Use these maps to plot military campaigns of the Revolutionary War, Civil War, and the War of 1812.

4. Plot highways, attractions, and national parks on the maps. Have students plan vacations to these areas and show their routes on the map. Students can write descriptions of those trips for sharing.

5. Create travel brochures for different states or regions.

Answer Key
Page 1: 1-7 consult an atlas or Milliken color transparency for answers 8. Arctic 9. Pacific 10. South America, Antarctica 11. southeast 12. east 13. North America 14. north 15. northern, western 16. Pacific 17. Indian 18. Cancer, Capricorn

Page 2: 1. consult an atlas 2. c, g, b, f, a, h, e, d 3. e, c, d, f, g, b, h, a 4. consult an atlas 5a. T b. F c. T d. ? e. T f. ? 6. Pacific, Panama, Caribbean, Hispaniola, Atlantic, Newfoundland

Page 3: 19, 43, 48, 11, 37, 30, 10, 12, 46, 20, 49, 41, 24, 23, 27, 45, 14, 50, 4, 7, 8, 39, 26, 16, 25, 33, 40, 42, 2, 5, 38, 1, 17, 28, 21, 44, 35, 3, 9, 18, 22, 15, 36, 32, 6, 13, 34, 47, 29, 31

Page 4: consult an atlas or Milliken color transparency for answers

Page 5: 1. humid subtropical 2. tropical wet-dry 3. continental 4. subarctic 5. tundra 6. mediterranean 7. continental 8. steppe 9. 100-150 cm 10. 50-100 cm 11. desert, 0-50 cm 12. more, Sierra Nevada 13. marine west coast, yes 14. short growing season, little sunlight, poor climate 15. e 16. a 17. i 18. h 19. b 20. j 21. c 22. d 23. g 24. f

Page 6: 1. consult an encyclopedia or Milliken color transparency for answers 2. Washington, Oregon, Idaho 3. California, Nevada, Utah, Arizona, also Colorado and New Mexico 4. 1842 5. North Dakota, Minnesota

Page 7:
1. N   11. N   21. N   31. S   41. N

2. N	12. A	22. N	32. E	42. N
3. N	13. N	23. N	33. E	43. N
4. N	14. A	24. N	34. N	44. N
5. S	15. N	25. N	35. N	45. F
6. S	16. N	26. S	36. N	46. E
7. N	17. N	27. N	37. F	47. A
8. E	18. F	28. S	38. E	48. E
9. S	19. F, E	29. E	39. D	49. N
10. E	20. E	30. E	40. E	50. N

Page 8: 1-2 consult an atlas or Milliken color transparency for answers 3. 0-2 sq. km 4. 2-20 sq. km 5. 2-20 sq. km 6. 20-40 sq. km 7. 40-100 km 8. F 9. T 10. F 11. F 12. St. Louis 13. Chicago, Milwaukee 14. Atlanta 15. Philadelphia 16. Boston 17. Los Angeles 18. Seattle 19. Denver 20. New Orleans 21. Miami 22. Buffalo 23. Phoenix 24. Washington, D.C. 25. Pittsburgh

Page 9: 1. east, Cincinnati 2. southwest, Atlanta 3. west, Denver, Salt Lake City, Cheyenne 4. southeast or east, Phoenix, San Antonio or El Paso 5. Bismarck 6. St. Louis, New Orleans (also accept Minneapolis and Memphis) 7. Pittsburgh, Cincinnati 8. Nashville 9. Portland 10. Hudson, Buffalo, Erie 11. Arkansas, Mississippi, Ohio 12. (choose five) Washington, Idaho, Montana, South Dakota, Minnesota, Wisconsin, Illinois, Indiana, Ohio, Pennsylvania, New York, Massachusetts 13. north south, (choose five) Maine, Florida, Massachusetts, Connecticut, New York, New Jersey, Pennsylvania, Maryland, Virginia, North Carolina, South Carolina, Georgia 14. 55, 70, 25 15. 5, 10, 35

Page 10: 1-4 consult an atlas or Milliken color transparency for answers 5. east 6. Augusta, 220 km, east, Vermont 7. Delaware, Delaware, Atlantic, Chesapeake, Potomac 8. southwest 9. southwest, 910 km, Connecticut, Hudson, Delaware, Susquehanna 10. west, Green 11. Chesapeake 12. Connecticut 13. Philadelphia 14. Appalachian 15. Boston

Page 11: 1-4 consult an atlas or Milliken color transparency for answers

Page 12: 1-4 consult an atlas or Milliken color transparency for answers 5. Michigan 6. south 7. 300 km, west 8. south, 375 km, Illinois or Wisconsin 9. south, 350 km 10. Michigan, Huron, St. Clair, Erie 11. Indianapolis 12. Great 13. Madison 14. Michigan 15. Cincinnati 16. Chicago, south 17. Ohio, Indiana, Illinois 18. Detroit 19. Wabash 20. Chicago, Detroit

Page 13: 1-4 consult an atlas or Milliken color transparency for answers

Page 14: 1-4 consult an atlas or Milliken color transparency for answers 5. west 1060 km, Pecos, Brazos 6. Colorado, north 7. Rio Grande 8. 400 km, west 9. Canadian, Arkansas 10. Llano Estacado 11. Pecos, New Mexico 12. Ouachita 13. Red 14. Arizona 15. Phoenix, 500,000-999,999 16. Rio Grande 17. Austin, south 18. New Mexico 19. Texas 20. Houston

Page 15: 1-5 consult an atlas or Milliken color transparency for answers 6. 475 km, southwest 7. west, Rocky, Colorado, Green, Wasatch 8. southwest 9. Bitterroot 10. Great Plains 11. Great Basin, Wheeler 12. Great Plains 13. Denver 14. Great Salt 15. Snake 16. Nevada 17. Missouri 18. Rocky 19. Wyoming 20. Colorado

Page 16: 1-5 consult an atlas or Milliken color transparency for answers

© Milliken Publishing Company

The United States in the World

Use the maps and additional references to complete the following.

1. Label and color the continents.

Africa	green
Asia	orange
Europe	yellow
Australia	red
North America	brown
South America	purple
Antarctica	gray

2. Label these parallels and meridians: Equator, Tropic of Cancer, Tropic of Capricorn, Arctic Circle, Antarctic Circle, and Prime Meridian.

3. Label the North and South poles. Label the four hemispheres.

4. Label the oceans: Pacific, Atlantic, Indian, and Arctic.

5. Label the compass rose on the map with these directions: north, south, east, west, northeast, southeast, northwest, and southwest.

6. Label the United States of America.

7. Label the countries north and south of the United States.

Use the eight major directions or names of oceans and continents to complete the statements.

8. The _____ Ocean is north of the United States.

9. The _____ Ocean lies to the west of the United States.

10. The continents of _____ and _____ lie south of the United States.

11. The continent of Africa lies _____ of the United States.

12. The Atlantic Ocean lies _____ of the United States.

13. The United States is part of the continent of _____.

14. The United States lies _____ of South America.

15. The United States is in the _____ and _____ hemispheres.

16. Asia is west of the United States and across the _____ Ocean.

17. None of the United States borders the _____ Ocean.

18. Most of the United States lies north of the Tropic of _____. All of the

   United States lies north of the Tropic of _____.

The United States in the World

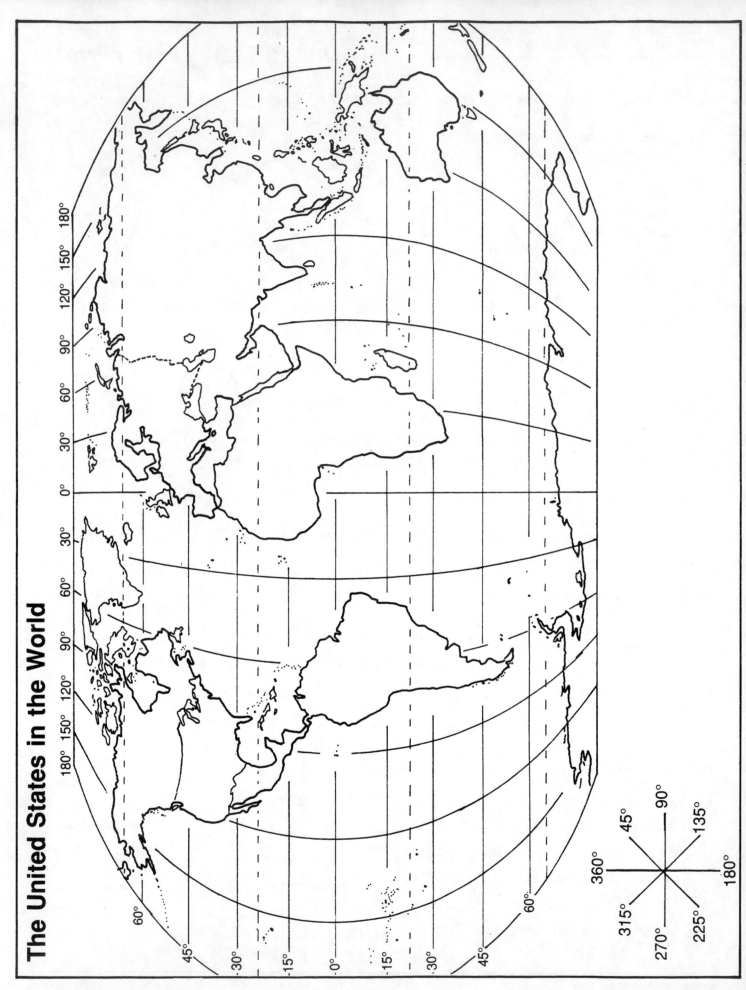

North America

Use the maps or additional references to complete the following.

1. Label the Arctic Ocean, Atlantic Ocean, and Pacific Ocean.

2. Label these bodies of water and match them with their latitudes and longitudes.

_____	Hudson Bay	a.	70°N	60°W
_____	Gulf of Mexico	b.	15°N	75°W
_____	Caribbean Sea	c.	60°N	90°W
_____	Gulf of St. Lawrence	d.	09°N	80°W
_____	Baffin Bay	e.	58°N	145°W
_____	Beaufort Sea	f.	48°N	62°W
_____	Gulf of Alaska	g.	25°N	90°W
_____	Panama Canal	h.	72°N	140°W

3. Label these islands and match them with their latitudes and longitudes.

_____	Cuba	a.	70°N	110°W
_____	Jamaica	b.	18°N	67°W
_____	Hispaniola	c.	18°N	78°W
_____	Greenland	d.	18°N	73°W
_____	Baffin Island	e.	22°N	80°W
_____	Puerto Rico	f.	70°N	40°W
_____	Newfoundland	g.	70°N	72°W
_____	Victoria Island	h.	49°N	56°W

4. Label these countries: Mexico, United States, Canada, Panama, Cuba, Nicaragua, Costa Rica, Dominican Republic, and Bahamas.

5. Using map 2a, answer the following statements as true or false. If you cannot answer from the map, put a question mark to indicate that not enough information is given.

   _____ Baffin Bay is west of Greenland.
   _____ The Caribbean Sea lies southwest of the Gulf of Mexico.
   _____ Haiti is on the same island as the Dominican Republic.
   _____ Lake Superior is larger than Great Bear Lake.
   _____ The Gulf of St. Lawrence is just west of Newfoundland.
   _____ Victoria Island is larger than Ellesmere Island.

6. To sail from a city on the Gulf of Alaska to a city on the Gulf of St. Lawrence a ship would

   probably have to go south and southeast across the _____ Ocean, through the

   _____ Canal, north across the _____ Sea, between the islands of

   Cuba and _____, into the _____ Ocean, and then between the North

   American mainland and the island of _____ to reach its destination.

North America

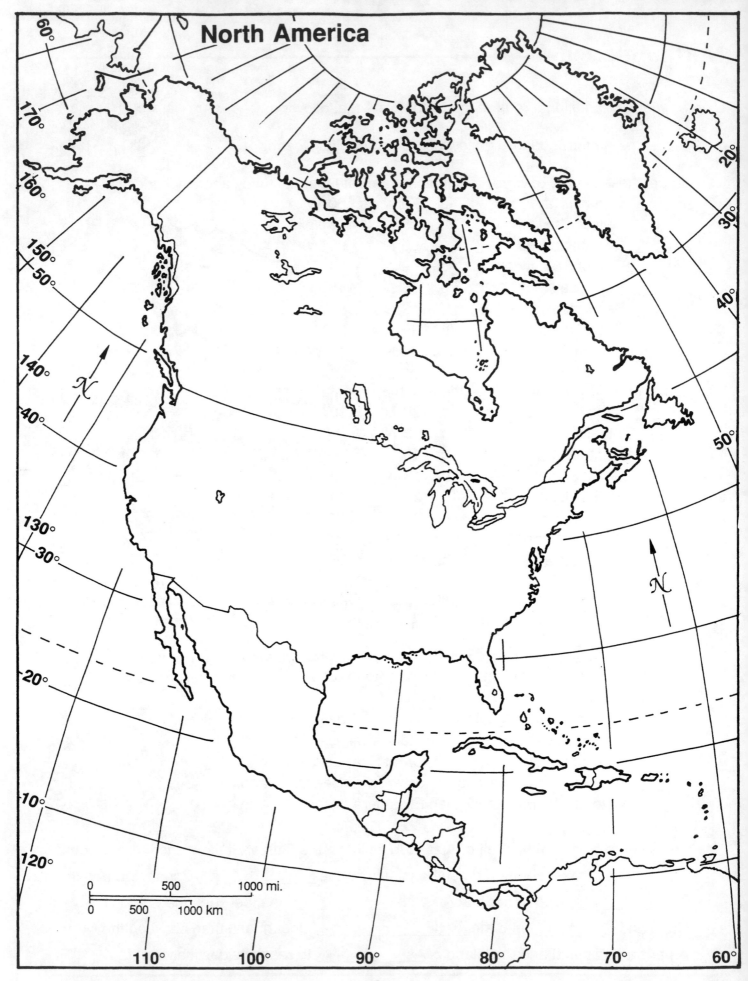

© Milliken Publishing Company

Map Skills—United States

Match each state with its capital city. Label the states on the map.

_____	Alabama		1.	Albany
_____	Alaska		2.	Concord
_____	Arizona		3.	Harrisburg
_____	Arkansas		4.	Augusta
_____	California		5.	Trenton
_____	Colorado		6.	Montpelier
_____	Connecticut		7.	Annapolis
_____	Delaware		8.	Boston
_____	Florida		9.	Providence
_____	Georgia		10.	Hartford
_____	Hawaii		11.	Little Rock
_____	Idaho		12.	Dover
_____	Illinois		13.	Richmond
_____	Indiana		14.	Frankfort
_____	Iowa		15.	Nashville
_____	Kansas		16.	Jackson
_____	Kentucky		17.	Raleigh
_____	Louisiana		18.	Columbia
_____	Maine		19.	Montgomery
_____	Maryland		20.	Atlanta
_____	Massachusetts		21.	Columbus
_____	Michigan		22.	Pierre
_____	Minnesota		23.	Indianapolis
_____	Mississippi		24.	Springfield
_____	Missouri		25.	Jefferson City
_____	Montana		26.	St. Paul
_____	Nebraska		27.	Des Moines
_____	Nevada		28.	Bismarck
_____	New Hampshire		29.	Madison
_____	New Jersey		30.	Denver
_____	New Mexico		31.	Cheyenne
_____	New York		32.	Salt Lake City
_____	North Carolina		33.	Helena
_____	North Dakota		34.	Olympia
_____	Ohio		35.	Salem
_____	Oklahoma		36.	Austin
_____	Oregon		37.	Sacramento
_____	Pennsylvania		38.	Santa Fe
_____	Rhode Island		39.	Lansing
_____	South Carolina		40.	Lincoln
_____	South Dakota		41.	Boise
_____	Tennessee		42.	Carson City
_____	Texas		43.	Juneau
_____	Utah		44.	Oklahoma City
_____	Vermont		45.	Topeka
_____	Virginia		46.	Tallahassee
_____	Washington		47.	Charleston
_____	West Virginia		48.	Phoenix
_____	Wisconsin		49.	Honolulu
_____	Wyoming		50.	Baton Rouge

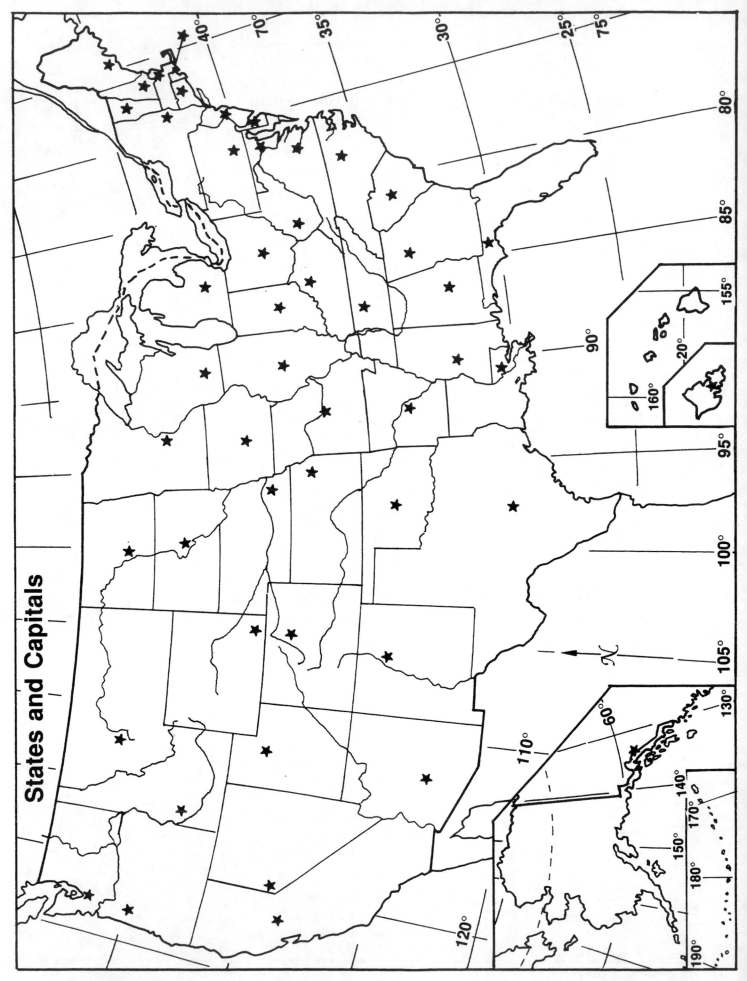

States and Capitals

Physical Features

Read the following paragraphs and label the **boldfaced** physical features on the map. You may consult previous maps for more information.

These major bodies of water surround the United States: **Atlantic Ocean, Arctic Ocean, Pacific Ocean,** and the **Gulf of Mexico.** The United States has great access to the world's oceans through: **Chesapeake Bay** 38°N, 76°W, **Delaware Bay** 39°N, 75°W, **Mobile Bay** 30°N, 88°W, **Galveston Bay** 30°N, 95°W, **Puget Sound** 48°N, 123°W, and **San Francisco Bay** 38°N, 122°W.

The **Rocky Mountains** run north and south across the western United States. The **Sierra Nevada** run north and south along eastern California. Along the Pacific coast from California to Washington are the **Coast Ranges.** East of the Coast Ranges in Oregon and Washington are the **Cascade Mountains.** The **Brooks Range** crosses northern Alaska, and the **High Alaska Range** crosses southern Alaska. Running northeast from Georgia to Maine are the **Appalachian Mountains.** In eastern Oklahoma and western Arkansas are the **Ouachita Mountains.** Northeast of them, in northern Arkansas and southern Missouri, is the **Ozark Plateau.** The **Colorado Plateau** is in the "four corners" region where Utah, Colorado, Arizona, and New Mexico meet. The **Columbia Plateau** covers much of eastern Oregon.

The area between the Coast Ranges and the Sierra Nevada, the Central Valley of California, is often called the **San Joaquin Valley.** East of the Sierra Nevada is the **Great Basin.** Much of the Great Basin is a desert. The section of the basin just west of the Great Salt Lake is called the **Great Salt Lake Desert.** The **Mojave Desert** is in extreme southeast California and the **Sonoran Desert** is in southern Arizona.

East of the Rocky Mountains, from Canada to Texas, is the **Great Plains.** The **Central Plains** cover much of Illinois, Indiana, and Ohio. The **Coastal Plains** extend along the Gulf of Mexico and southern Atlantic coasts from Texas to Virginia.

There are many large lakes in the United States: **Lake Ontario** 44°N, 78°W, **Lake Erie** 42°N, 81°W, **Lake Superior** 48°N, 90°W, **Lake Michigan** 43°N, 87°W, **Lake Huron** 45°N, 83°W, and the **Great Salt Lake** 41°N, 113°W.

There are many large and useful rivers in the United States. The **Hudson River** flows south through the state of New York. The **Columbia River** flows from Canada through Washington to the Pacific Ocean. Its largest tributary, the **Snake River,** flows through Idaho and Washington. The **Colorado River** flows from Wyoming and Colorado to its mouth in Mexico. The **Rio Grande** flows from the Colorado River south through New Mexico and then forms the Mexican border as it flows southeast to the Gulf of Mexico. The **Yukon River** rises in northwest Canada and flows west through Alaska to the Pacific Ocean.

Many of the lower 48 states lie within the Mississippi River Drainage Basin. The **Mississippi River** flows from Minnesota south to the Gulf of Mexico. Its longest tributary, the **Missouri River,** flows from Montana to its mouth in Missouri. The **Platte River** flows from Wyoming and Colorado east through Nebraska. The **Ohio River** carries more water than any other Mississippi tributary; it flows southwest from its head in Pennsylvania.

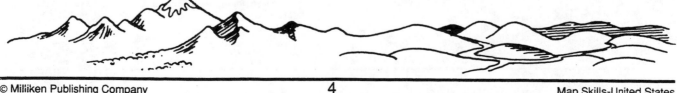

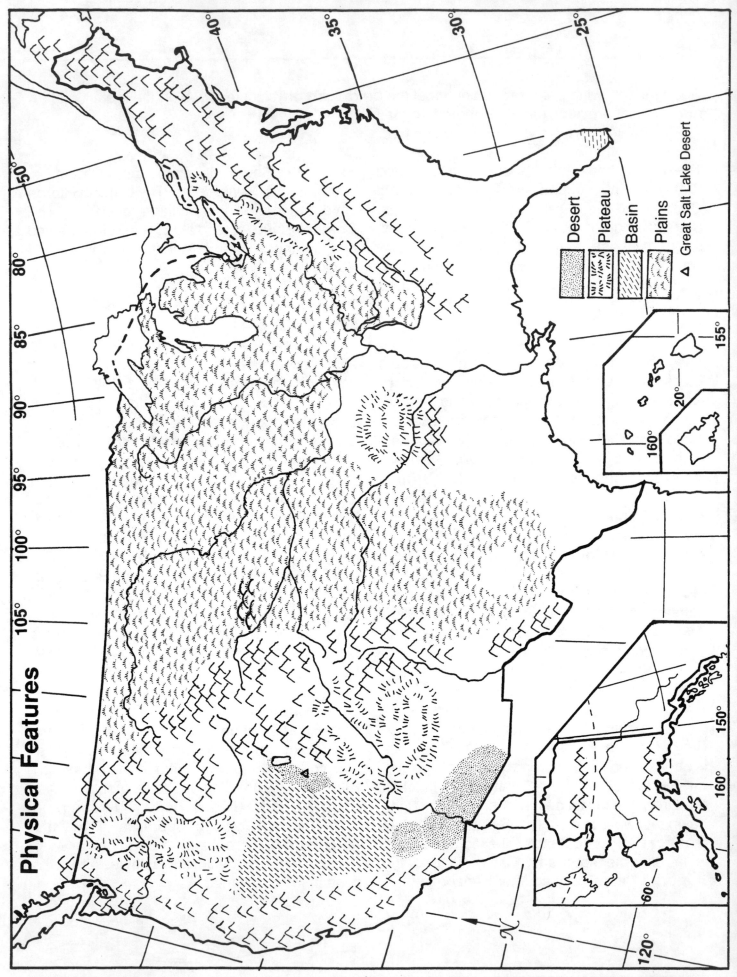

Physical Features

Desert
Plateau
Basin
Plains
△ Great Salt Lake Desert

© Milliken Publishing Company

4a

Use the maps to complete the following.

List the climate type for:

1. most of the southeastern states _____
2. the southern tip of Florida _____
3. the northeastern states _____
4. most of Alaska _____
5. northern Alaska _____
6. most of southern California _____
7. the eastern Great Plains _____
8. the western Great Plains _____

9. Most of the humid subtropical areas of the southeastern states receive between _____ and _____ cm of rain.

10. Most of the area around the western Great Lakes receives _____ to _____ cm of rain.

11. Much of the Great Basin has a _____ climate and receives _____ to _____ cm of rain.

12. Most of California receives _____ rain than the Great Basin. What physiographic feature prevents moist air from reaching the Great Basin? _____

13. The west coasts of Washington, Oregon, and southeast Alaska have a _____ climate. Do they receive a great deal of rain? _____

14. Give two reasons why few crops are grown in Alaska. _____
_____

Match the climate types and their descriptions.

15. _____ tropical wet   a. hot dry summers, cold winters, light rain
16. _____ semi-arid   b. hot summers, cool winters
17. _____ desert   c. warm summers, cold winters
18. _____ mediterranean   d. cool summers, cold winters, little rain
19. _____ humid subtropical   e. hot all year, heavy rain
20. _____ marine   f. varies with elevation
21. _____ continental   g. cool summers, very cold winters, no trees
22. _____ subarctic   h. hot and dry summers, cool wet winters
23. _____ tundra   i. hot summers, dry winters, very little rain
24. _____ highlands   j. warm summers, cool winters, heavy precipitation

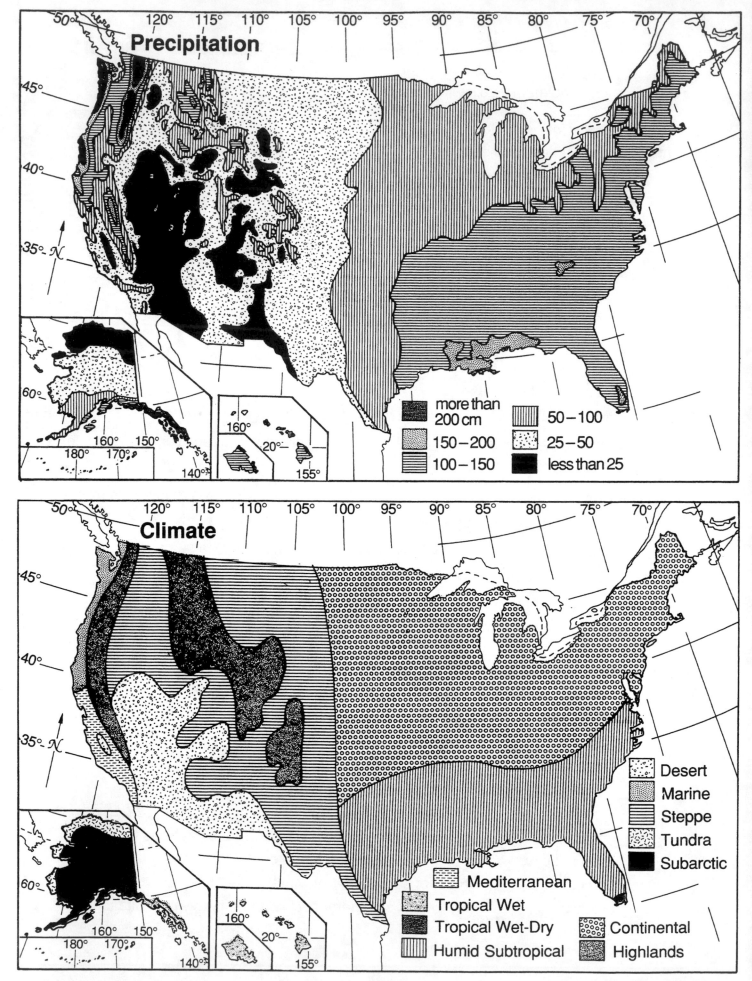

Precipitation

	more than 200 cm		50 – 100
	150 – 200		25 – 50
	100 – 150		less than 25

Climate

Desert
Marine
Steppe
Tundra
Subarctic

Mediterranean
Tropical Wet
Tropical Wet-Dry
Humid Subtropical
Continental
Highlands

© Milliken Publishing Company

Map Skills–United States

Expansion of the American Republic

Read the following paragraphs and use the information to answer the questions.

The original thirteen colonies (plus most of the territories that were to become Vermont and Maine) fought for independence in the Revolutionary War of 1776-1781. As part of the Treaty of Paris of 1783, Great Britain also ceded the lands west of the colonies to the Mississippi River.

In 1803 the U.S. bought land known as the Louisiana Purchase from France, which included much of the rest of the Mississippi-Missouri Basin. From 1810-1813 the U.S. obtained parts of western Florida from the Spanish. After reasserting itself as a nation in the war of 1812, the U.S. signed a treaty with Great Britain (1818) establishing the Canadian border at 49° north. The U.S. gave up lands in the Missouri headwaters and Great Britain gave up the Red River Basin. Realizing the power of the U.S., Spain sold eastern Florida to the U.S. in 1821.

In 1836 Mexicans and Americans in Texas defeated forces of Mexico and declared Texas an independent nation. In 1842 the U.S. and Great Britain signed another treaty establishing the northern borders of what is now Minnesota and Maine; each country gained and lost land. In 1845 Congress approved statehood for Texas and it was annexed. This led to war with Mexico and the Bear Flag Revolt in California against Mexican rule. This war ended in 1847 when U.S. forces captured the Mexican capital, Mexico City. The treaty of 1848 ceded large amounts of Mexican land in what is now southwestern U.S. Just prior to this war (in 1846) the U.S. and Great Britain signed another treaty extending the 49th parallel border all the way to the Pacific Ocean. This created the Oregon Territory. In 1853 the U.S. purchased land (Gadsden Purchase) in what is now southern Arizona from Mexico.

After the Civil War in 1867, the U.S. purchased Alaska from Russia. This was unpopular with many people who could not imagine the value of the northern land. In 1893 American and European planters and others deposed the queen of the Hawaiian Islands, established a republic, and applied for admission to the U.S. as a territory; this offer was accepted by Congress in 1898. War with the Spanish resulted in these areas being ceded to the U.S. in 1898: Philippine Islands, Cuba, Puerto Rico, and Guam. Independence came to Cuba in 1901 and to the Philippines in 1946. The Virgin Islands were purchased from Denmark in 1917.

1. Label on the map: thirteen colonies, Treaty of Paris lands, Louisiana Purchase, western Florida, Red River Basin, eastern Florida, northern Maine, Texas, Oregon Territory, Treaty of 1848 lands, Gadsden Purchase, Alaska, and Hawaii.

2. Name three states gained by treaty in 1846. _____

_____

3. Name four states obtained completely or partially by the Mexican War Treaty of 1848.

_____

4. Part of Maine was included in the original states and part was obtained in _____.

5. Most of the Red River Basin lands ceded by Great Britain in 1818 are now parts of what

   two states? _____

6

Expansion of the American Republic

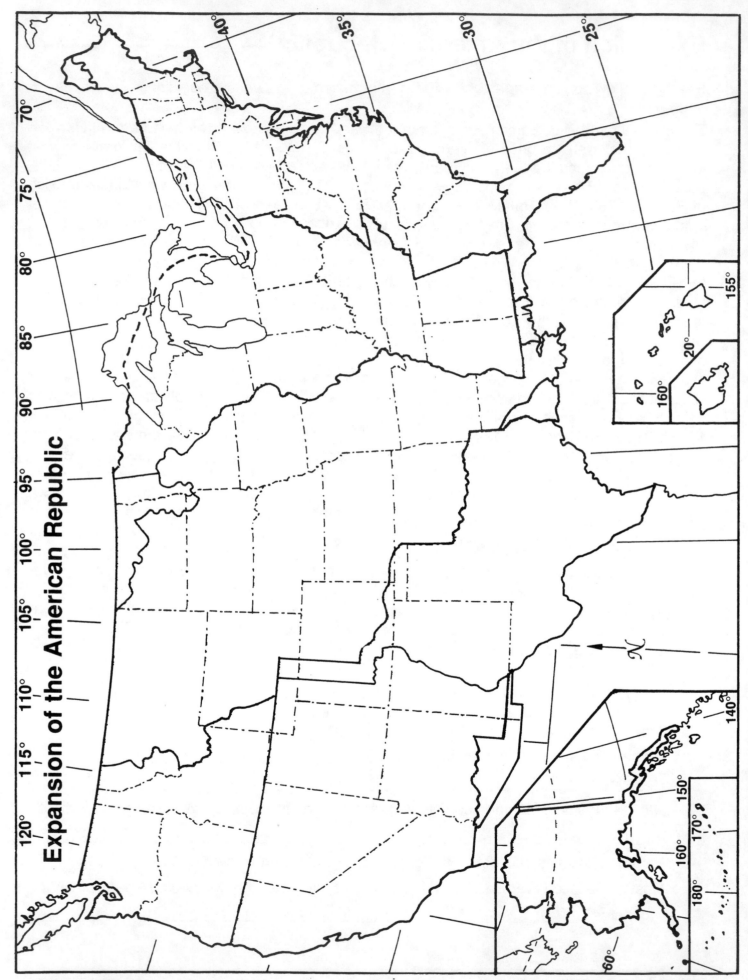

© Milliken Publishing Company

Map Skills—United States

Origins of State Names

Classify the state names as to their origins using the key below. Color code the map.

		Key	
D	Dutch		grey
E	English		orange
F	French		blue
N	Native American		green
S	Spanish		red
A	American		yellow

1. _____ Alabama — Alibama: "Clear the Woods"
2. _____ Alaska — Alyeska: "Great Land"
3. _____ Arizona — Arizona: "Springs"
4. _____ Arkansas — Arkansa: "Downstream"
5. _____ California — California, fictional island
6. _____ Colorado — Colorado: "Color Red"
7. _____ Connecticut — Connecticut: "Along Tidal River"
8. _____ Delaware — Thomas West, Lord De la Warre
9. _____ Florida — Florida: "Flowers"
10. _____ Georgia — King George II
11. _____ Hawaii — Hawaii, original homeland
12. _____ Idaho — coined phrase (?): "Gem"
13. _____ Illinois — Iliniwek: "Superior Men"
14. _____ Indiana — Land of Indians
15. _____ Iowa — Iowa tribe
16. _____ Kansas — Kansa: "People of South Wind"
17. _____ Kentucky — Kenta-Ke: "Grassland"
18. _____ Louisiana — King Louis XIV
19. _____ Maine — province of Maine, or mainland
20. _____ Maryland — queen consort Henrietta Maria
21. _____ Massachusetts — Massachuset: "At Great Hill"
22. _____ Michigan — Mesikami: "Great Lake"
23. _____ Minnesota — Minisota: "Sky-Color Waters"
24. _____ Mississippi — Misi-sipi: "Great River"
25. _____ Missouri — Missouri: "People of the Big Canoes"
26. _____ Montana — Montana: "Mountainous"
27. _____ Nebraska — Nebrathka: "Flat Water"
28. _____ Nevada — Nevada: "Snow Covered"
29. _____ New Hampshire — county of Hampshire
30. _____ New Jersey — island of Jersey
31. _____ New Mexico — land of Mexico
32. _____ New York — duke or city of York
33. _____ North Carolina — King Charles (carolus in Latin)
34. _____ North Dakota — Dakota: "Allies"
35. _____ Ohio — Oheo: "Lovely or Great"
36. _____ Oklahoma — Okla-humma: "Red People Land"
37. _____ Oregon — possibly Ouragan: "Hurricane"
38. _____ Pennsylvania — William Penn, founder's father
39. _____ Rhode Island — Rhod "Red" Island
40. _____ South Carolina — King Charles (carolus in Latin)
41. _____ South Dakota — Dakota: "Allies"
42. _____ Tennessee — village of Tenase
43. _____ Texas — Tehas: "Friends"
44. _____ Utah — Ute tribe
45. _____ Vermont — Vert Mont: "Green Mountain"
46. _____ Virginia — Queen Elizabeth, the virgin queen
47. _____ Washington — George Washington
48. _____ West Virginia — Queen Elizabeth, the virgin queen
49. _____ Wisconsin — Wishkonsing: "Home of Owners"
50. _____ Wyoming — Wa-Wo-Mah: "Great Plains"

© Milliken Publishing Company

Map Skills-United States

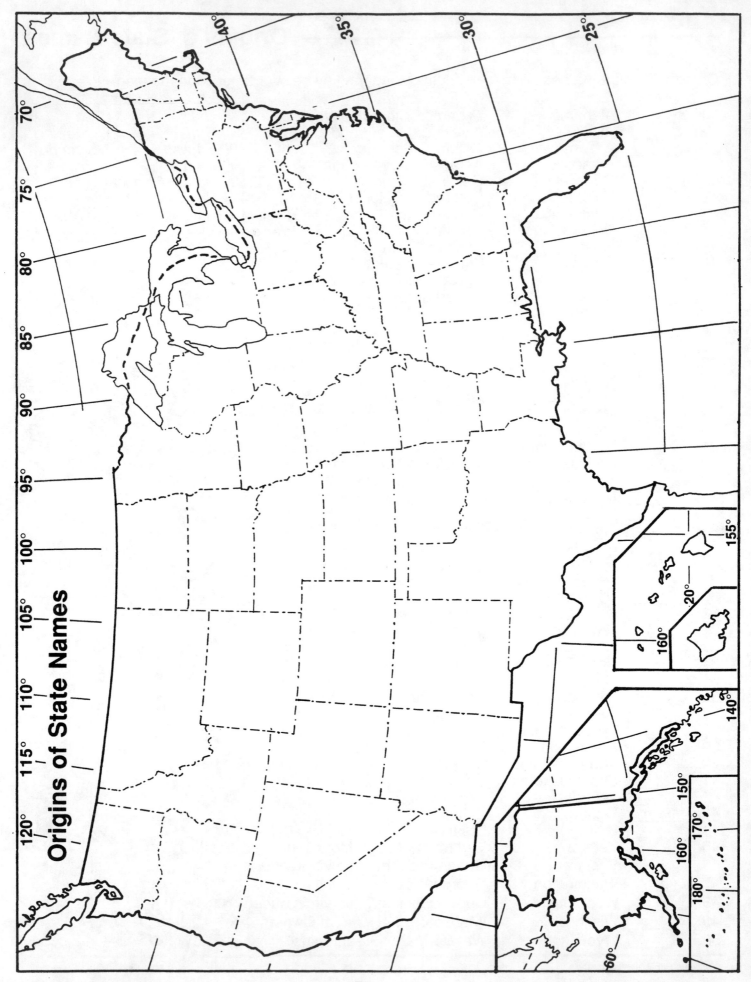

Origins of State Names

© Milliken Publishing Company

7a

Map Skills–United States

Population Density and Large Cities

1. Label these cities and metropolitan areas of over two million people: New York, Los Angeles, Chicago, San Francisco/Oakland, Philadelphia, Detroit, Boston, Dallas/Fort Worth, Washington, D.C., Houston, Miami/Fort Lauderdale, Cleveland/Akron, Atlanta, St. Louis, Seattle/Tacoma, Minneapolis/St. Paul, Baltimore, Pittsburgh, San Diego, Tampa/St. Petersburg, and Phoenix.

2. Label these cities and metropolitan areas of one to two million people: Denver, Cincinnati, Milwaukee, Kansas City, Portland, Norfolk/Virginia Beach, Sacramento, New Orleans, Columbus, San Antonio, Indianapolis, Buffalo, Providence, Charlotte, Hartford, Salt Lake City, Rochester, Memphis, Oklahoma City, and Nashville.

Give the population density:

3. for most of Nevada _____

4. for southwest Missouri _____

5. just south of Atlanta _____

6. along most of the Ohio River _____

7. in the Los Angeles area _____

True or False?

8. _____ North Carolina's heaviest population is along the Atlantic coast.

9. _____ Most of Minnesota's population lives in the central part of the state.

10. _____ Idaho is more densely populated than South Carolina.

11. _____ Large areas of low population lie between Baltimore and Boston.

Use the maps and additional references to complete the following.

12. Name the city where the Missouri and Mississippi rivers join. _____

13. Name two large cities on Lake Michigan. _____

14. What is the capital of Georgia? _____

15. What city is near 40°N and 75°W? _____

16. What city is east of 75°W and north of 42°N? _____

17. What city's name means the "city of angels?" _____

18. Name a large city on Puget Sound. _____

19. What city lies just east of the Rocky Mountains and north of 37°N? _____

20. What city is located along the Mississippi River near the Gulf of Mexico? _____

21. What city is south of 27°N and east of 82°W? _____

22. What city is located along the eastern edge of Lake Erie? _____

23. Name a city near the Sonoran Desert. _____

24. What city is the nation's capital? _____

25. Name the city at the head of the Ohio River. _____

Population Density and Large Cities

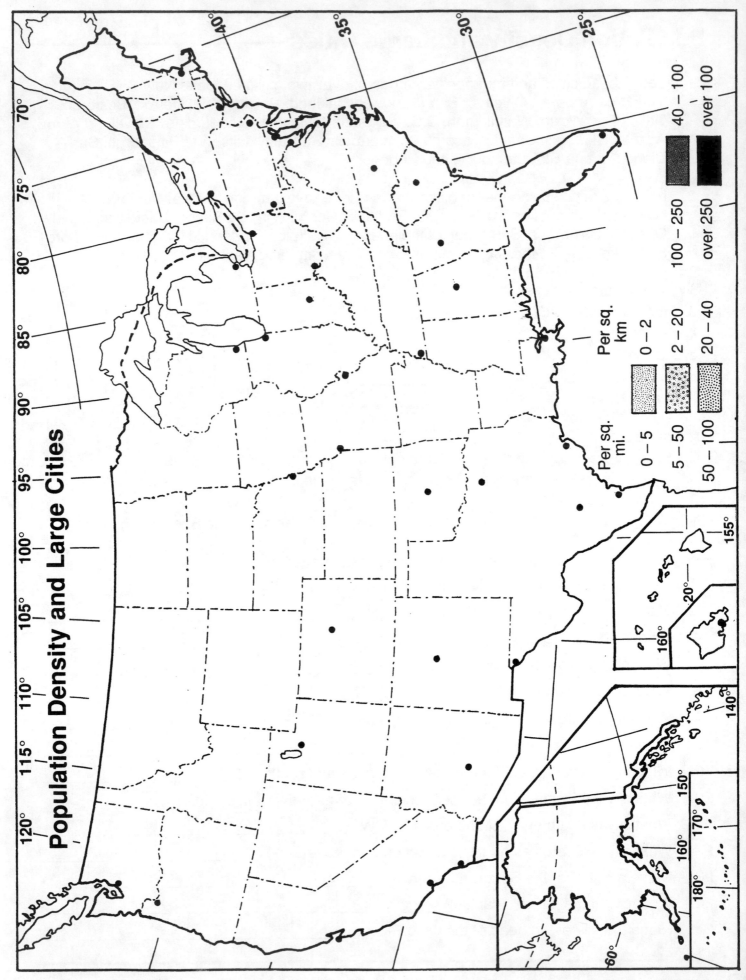

Per sq. mi.	Per sq. km
0 – 5	0 – 2
5 – 50	2 – 20
50 – 100	20 – 40
100 – 250	40 – 100
over 250	over 100

© Milliken Publishing Company

8a

─────────────────────────── **Transportation**

Use the maps or additional references to complete the following.

Railroads

1. When traveling by train from St. Louis to Norfolk you would go mostly _____ and through the city of _____ , Ohio.

2. Traveling by train from Washington, D.C. to New Orleans would take you in a _____ direction and you would pass through the city of _____ , Georgia.

3. To go from Chicago to San Francisco by train you would go mostly _____ and pass through the city of _____ Colorado and either _____ , Utah or _____ , Wyoming.

4. Traveling by train from San Diego to Houston would take you _____ through the cities of _____ , Arizona, and _____ , Texas.

5. The shortest route from Chicago to Seattle will take you through _____ , North Dakota.

Rivers

6. Name two cities that are probably ports on the Mississippi River. _____

   _____

7. Name two large cities on the Ohio River. _____

8. Name a large city on the Cumberland River. _____

9. Name a port city on the Columbia River. _____

10. A ship can travel from New York City to Cleveland by way of the _____ River, through the city of _____ , New York, and Lake _____ .

11. Cities in Oklahoma can ship goods to Pittsburgh via the _____ River, the _____ River, and the _____ River.

Interstate Highways

12. Interstate 90 goes from Seattle to Boston. Name five states it goes through. _____

    _____

13. Interstate 95 runs in a _____ to _____ direction from Maine to Miami. Name five states it connects. _____

    _____

14. What interstate would you take to travel between St. Louis and New Orleans? _____ St. Louis and Denver? _____ Denver and Santa Fe? _____

15. What interstate connects Seattle and Los Angeles? _____ Los Angeles and San Antonio? _____ San Antonio and Minneapolis? _____

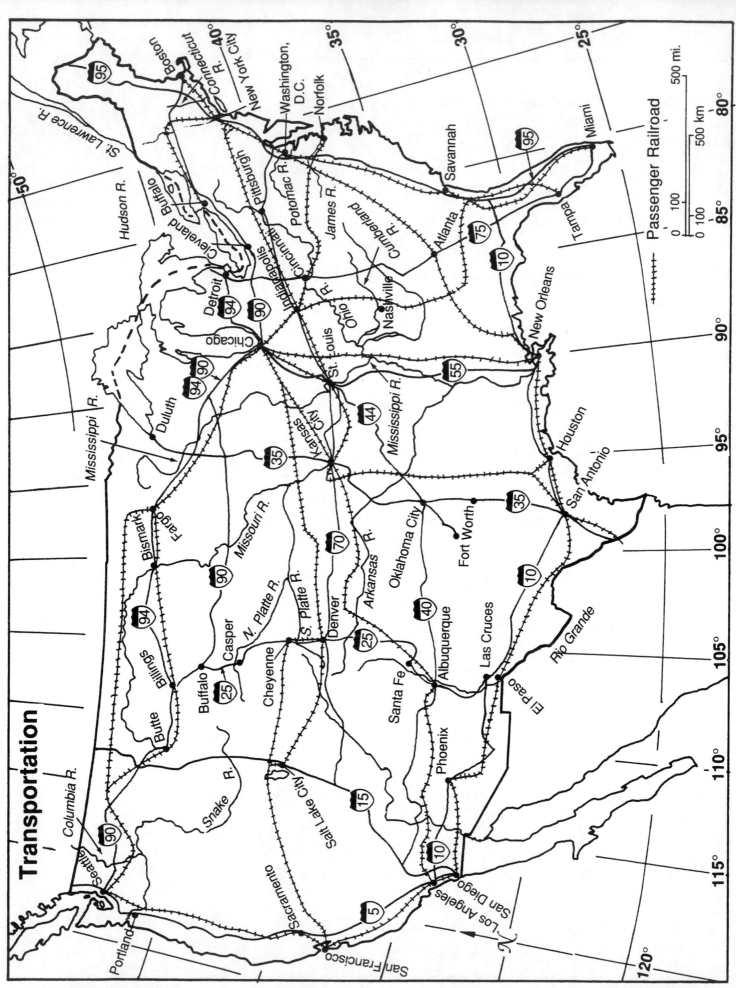

© Milliken Publishing Company

9a

The Northeastern States

Use previous maps or additional references to label the following.

1. Label the states and their capitals.
2. Label these features: White Mountains, Green Mountains, Adirondack Mountains, Appalachian Mountains, Mount Washington, Cape Cod, Niagara Falls, and Long Island.
3. Label these bodies of water: *Atlantic Ocean, Lake Ontario, Lake Erie, Hudson River, Potomac River, Delaware River, Ohio River, Lake Champlain, St. Lawrence River, St. John River, Penobscot River, Connecticut River, Allegheny River, Kanawha River, Delaware Bay,* and *Chesapeake Bay.*
4. Label these cities: New York City, Philadelphia, Buffalo, Rochester, Bangor, Portland, Manchester, Cambridge, Bridgeport, New Haven, Springfield, Atlantic City, Newark, Wilmington, Baltimore, Washington, D.C., Wheeling, Pittsburgh, Scranton, Erie, Syracuse, Burlington, and New Bedford.

Complete the following statements with distances, directions, and features.

5. Cape Cod lies _____ of most of Massachusetts.

6. The capital of Maine, _____, lies about _____ km/mi. _____ of Montpelier, the capital of _____.

7. A boat traveling from Philadelphia to the nation's capital would go down the _____ River, through _____ Bay, along the _____ Ocean coast, through _____ Bay, and up the _____ River.

8. Charleston is _____ of Harrisburg.

9. To fly from Augusta to Pittsburgh you go in a _____ direction for about _____ km/mi. and cross these four rivers: _____.

10. The Adirondack Mountains are _____ of the White Mountains and the_____ Mountains.

11. The Susquehanna and Potomac rivers empty into the _____ Bay.

12. The _____ River is a border for New Hampshire and Vermont and passes through Massachusetts and Connecticut.

13. The Declaration of Independence was signed in _____ (40°N, 75°W).

14. The Adirondacks, Catskills, and Alleghenies are all part of the _____ Mountain system.

15. _____ (42°N, 71°W) is known for a famous tea party.

The Northeastern States

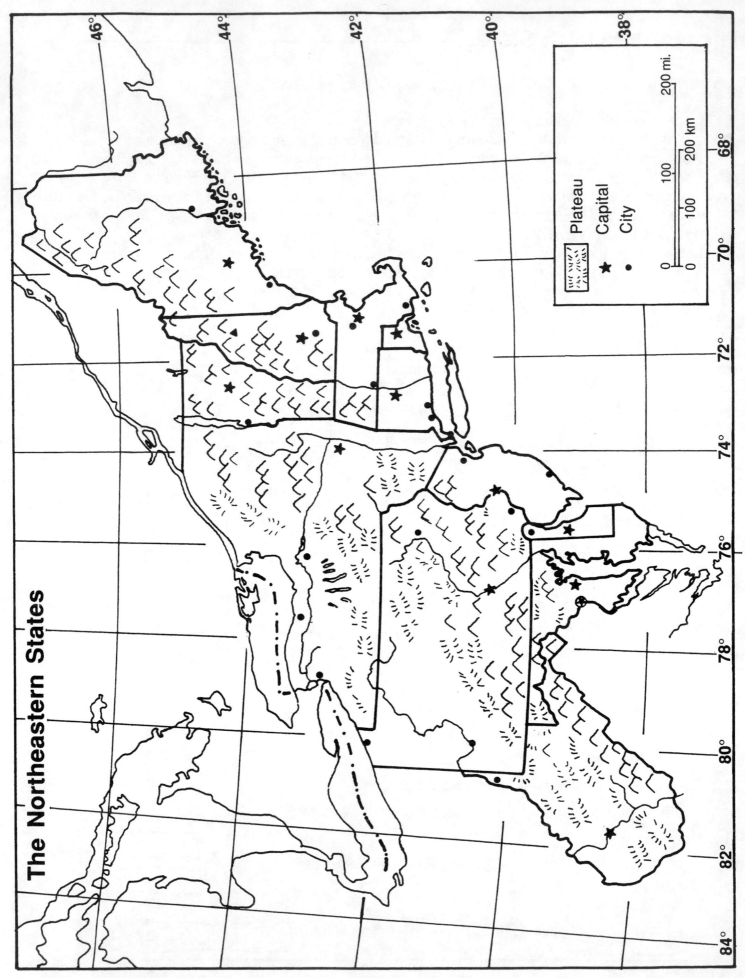

© Milliken Publishing Company

Map Skills–United States

Use previous maps or additional references to label the following.

1. Label the states and their capitals.
2. Label these features: Appalachian Mountains, Ouachita Mountains, the Everglades, Ozark Plateau, Cumberland Plateau, Blue Ridge Mountains, and Smoky Mountains.
3. Label these bodies of water: *Mississippi River, Atlantic Ocean, Gulf of Mexico, Ohio River, Tennessee River, Cumberland River, James River, Potomac River, Shenandoah River, Tampa Bay, Lake Okeechobee, Lake Pontchartrain, Oconee River,* and *Chattahoochee River.*
4. Label these cities: Charleston, Norfolk, Virginia Beach, Charlottesville, Louisville, Lexington, Knoxville, Chattanooga, Memphis, Charlotte, Huntsville, Birmingham, Biloxi, Fort Smith, Shreveport, New Orleans, Miami, Orlando, Tampa, St. Petersburg, Jacksonville, Greensboro, Mobile, Columbus, and Savannah.

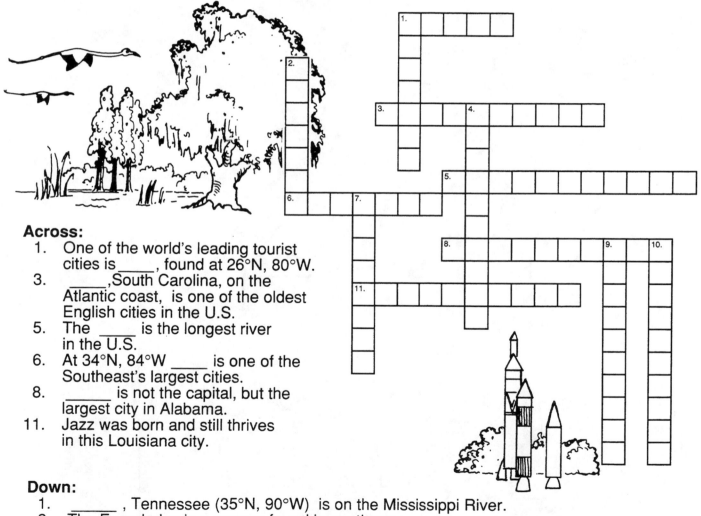

Across:
1. One of the world's leading tourist cities is _____, found at 26°N, 80°W.
3. _____, South Carolina, on the Atlantic coast, is one of the oldest English cities in the U.S.
5. The _____ is the longest river in the U.S.
6. At 34°N, 84°W _____ is one of the Southeast's largest cities.
8. _____ is not the capital, but the largest city in Alabama.
11. Jazz was born and still thrives in this Louisiana city.

Down:
1. _____, Tennessee (35°N, 90°W) is on the Mississippi River.
2. The Everglades is a swamp found in southern _____.
4. The Kentucky Derby is held in _____, Kentucky, found at 38°N, 86°W.
7. Hot Springs, _____ has a national park named for its 47 warm mineral springs.
9. _____, Alabama (35°N, 87°W) is the home of the Alabama Space and Rocket Center.
10. The highest peak of the Appalachians, found in North Carolina, is _____.

The Southeastern States

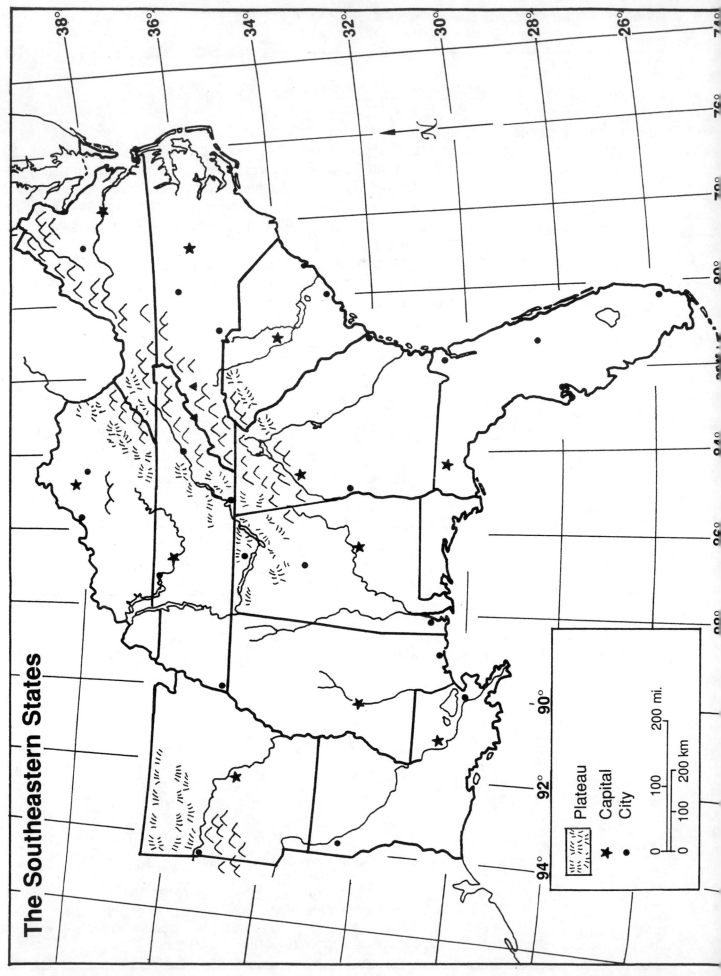

11a

Plateau

★ Capital

• City

200 mi.

200 km

0   100   200

The Great Lakes States ———————————————

Use previous maps or additional references to label the following.

1. Label the states and their capitals.
2. Label these features: Central Plains, Upper Peninsula, Door Peninsula, Mackinac Island, and Isle Royale.
3. Label these bodies of water: *Lake Superior, Lake Huron, Lake Michigan, Lake Erie, Ohio River, Mississippi River, Illinois River, Wabash River, Wisconsin River,* and *Lake St. Clair.*
4. Label these cities: Detroit, Chicago, Cleveland, Akron, Cincinnati, Toledo, Dayton, Milwaukee, Green Bay, Peoria, Rockford, Evansville, Fort Wayne, Gary, Grand Rapids, Ann Arbor, and Flint.

————————————————————————

Complete the following statements with distances, directions, and features.

5. Lake _____ separates Wisconsin and Lower Michigan.
6. Indiana lies _____ of Lake Michigan.
7. Springfield is _____ km/mi. _____ of Indianapolis.
8. If you flew from Madison to Springfield you would go _____ for _____ km/mi. and cross the _____ River.
9. Cincinnati is _____ of Cleveland and _____ km/mi. away.
10. To go from Chicago to Cleveland by water you would go through these four lakes:

    Lake _____, Lake _____, Lake _____, and

    Lake _____.
11. _____ is the capital of Indiana and the home of a famous car race.
12. The _____ Lakes are considered the largest group of freshwater lakes in the world.
13. The capital of Wisconsin is _____.
14. The Upper Peninsula is part of the state of _____.
15. The Hopewell Indians built a great mound outside of this Ohio city found at 39°N, 85°W.

    _____
16. _____, Illinois is found on Lake Michigan. It is located _____ of Milwaukee.
17. The Ohio River touches these states. _____
18. The _____ area of Michigan (42°N, 83°W) is known as the automobile capital of the world.
19. The _____ River forms a portion of the Indiana–Illinois border.
20. The two Great Lake cities with the greatest population are _____.

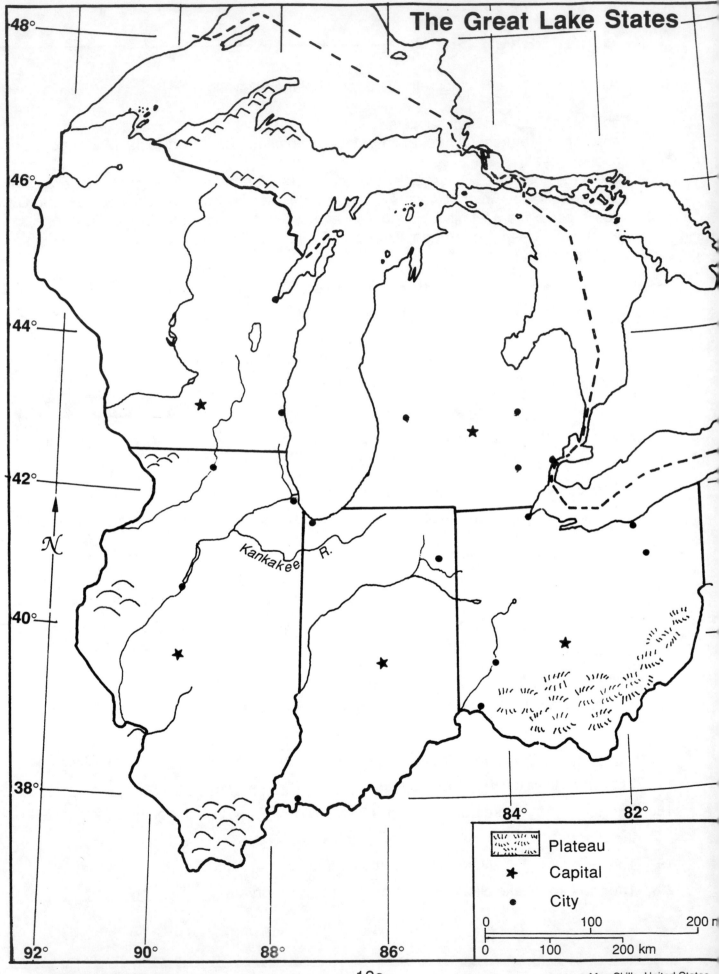

The Great Lake States

48°

46°

44°

42°

40°

38°

N

Kankakee R.

92°   90°   88°   86°   84°   82°

Plateau

Capital

City

0   100   200 m
0   100   200 km

© Milliken Publishing Company

12a

Map Skills—United States

Use previous maps or additional references to label the following.

1. Label the states and their capitals.
2. Label these features: Black Hills, Mesabi Range, and Ozark Plateau.
3. Label these bodies of water: *Mississippi River, Missouri River, Arkansas River, Platte River, Lake Superior, Red River, Republican River, Des Moines River, Minnesota River, Lake Sakakawea, Lake of the Woods,* and *James River.*
4. Label these cities: St. Louis, Kansas City, Minneapolis, Fargo, Sioux Falls, Rapid City, Grand Forks, Omaha, Grand Island, Springfield, St. Joseph, Independence, Columbia, Duluth, Rochester, International Falls, Wichita, Lawrence, Sioux City, Davenport, Waterloo, and Cedar Rapids.

Across:

2. Des Moines (42°N, 94°W) is the capital of ____.
3. Most of the Plains states are drained by the _____ River.
7. ____, Missouri and _____, Kansas are twin cities that lie on the Missouri River.
8. The ____ River flows north into Canada.

Down:

1. Minneapolis and St. Paul, ____ lie on opposite banks of the Mississippi River.
4. Mount Rushmore, found in the Black Hills, is located in_____.
5. The _____ River flows through southern Nebraska.
6. The _____ Plateau can be found in southern Missouri.

The Great Plains States

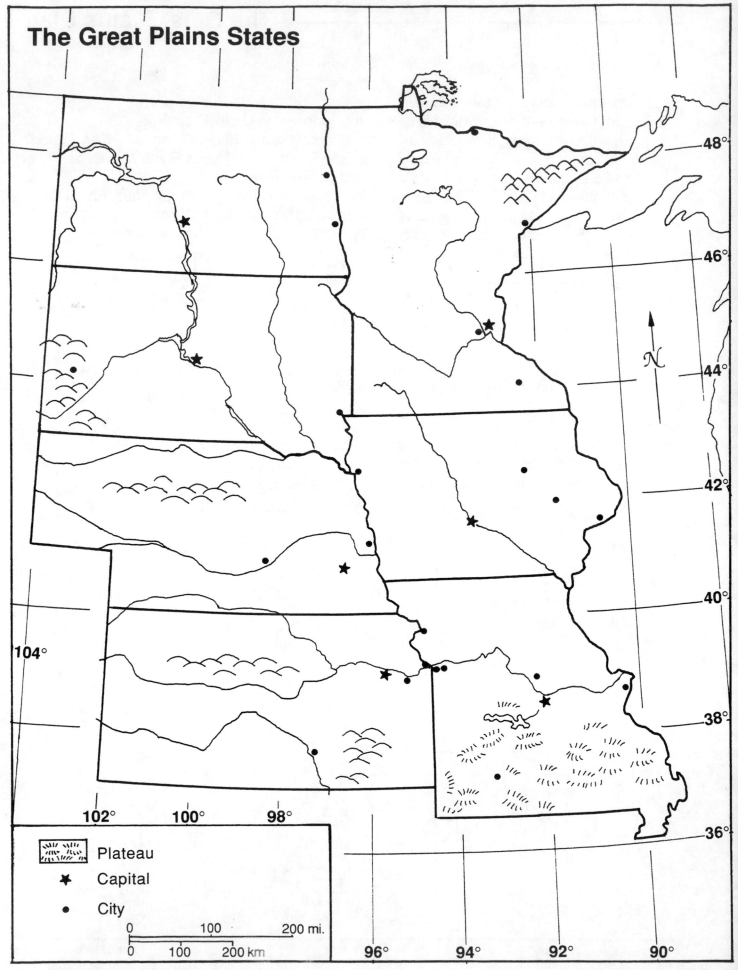

48°

46°

44°

42°

40°

104°

38°

36°

102°   100°   98°

Plateau

Capital

City

0   100   200 mi.

0   100   200 km

96°   94°   92°   90°

The Southwestern States

Use previous maps or additional references to label the features and to answer the questions.

1. Label the states and their capitals.
2. Label these features: Grand Canyon, Painted Desert, Colorado Plateau, Rocky Mountains, Great Plains, Truchas Peak, Sangre de Cristo Mountains, Santiago Mountains, Edwards Plateau, Llano Estacado, Sonoran Desert, Gulf of Mexico, Ouachita Mountains, and Guadalupe Mountains.
3. Label these bodies of water: *Colorado River, Rio Grande, Arkansas River, Gila River, Pecos River, Canadian River, Brazos River, Cimarron River, Little Colorado River,* and *Red River.*
4. Label these cities: Houston, Dallas, Fort Worth, San Antonio, Albuquerque, Tucson, Tulsa, El Paso, Corpus Christi, Las Cruces, Flagstaff, Amarillo, and Roswell.

Complete the following statements with distances, directions, and features.

5. To fly from Houston to El Paso you would go mostly _____ for _____ km/mi. and would cross these two rivers: _____.
6. The Grand Canyon was formed by the _____ River and lies _____ of Phoenix.
7. The _____, which flows from north to south, splits New Mexico in half.
8. Tucson lies about _____ km/mi. _____ of Las Cruces.
9. Oklahoma City lies between the _____ River and the _____ River.
10. The _____ is a large area of high, flat, dry land in northwestern Texas and eastern New Mexico.
11. The _____ River is a tributary of the Rio Grande and flows from_____ into Texas.
12. The _____ Mountains are north of the Red River in Oklahoma.
13. The _____ River borders Oklahoma and Texas.
14. Grand Canyon National Park (36°N, 112°W) is located in the state of_____.
15. The capital of Arizona, _____ is a growing city with a population of _____.
16. The _____ flows southeast into the Gulf of Mexico.
17. _____, the capital of Texas, lies _____ of Dallas.
18. Carlsbad Caverns National Park (32°N, 104°W) is located in the state of _____.
19. Once a fort, the Alamo is an important place in this state's history. _____.
20. This city located at 30°N, 95°W has a population over one million. _____

The Southwestern States

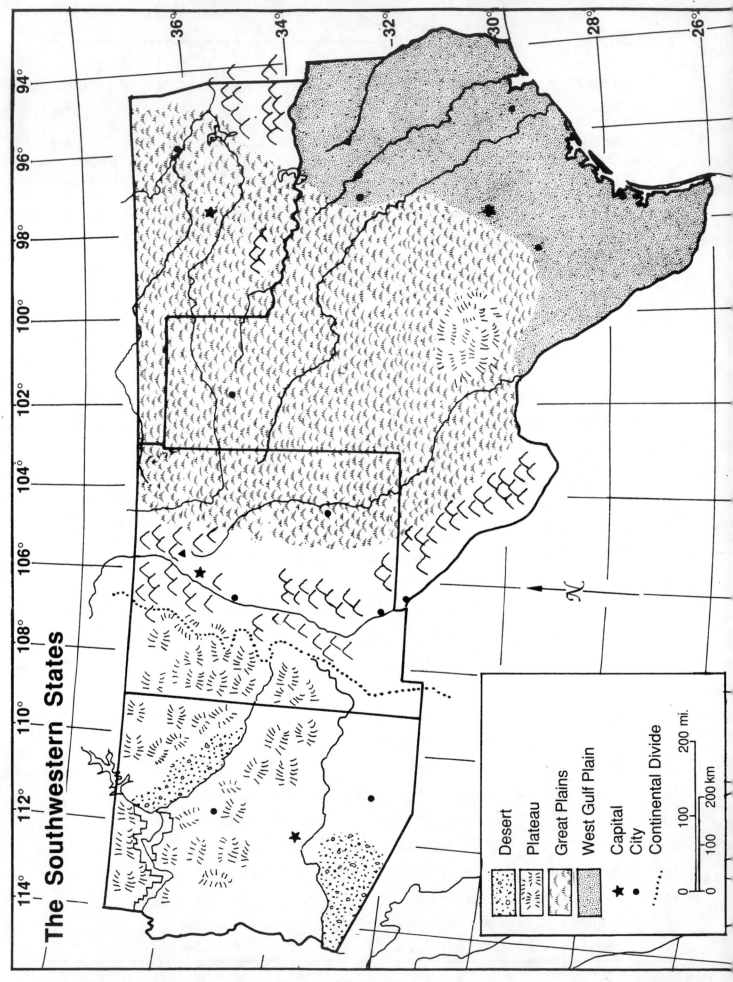

Desert
Plateau
Great Plains
West Gulf Plain
Capital
City
Continental Divide

0   100   200 mi.
0   100   200 km

Use previous maps or additional references to label the following.

1. Label the states and their capitals.
2. Label these features: Bitterroot Range, Wind River Range, Wasatch Range, Uinta Mountains, Front Range, Sangre de Cristo Mountains, Great Salt Lake Desert, Great Basin, Rocky Mountains, Colorado Plateau, Big Horn Mountains, Continental Divide, and Great Plains.
3. Label these bodies of water: *Arkansas River, Snake River, Colorado River, North Platte River, South Platte River, Missouri River, Great Salt Lake, Green River,* and *Yellowstone River.*
4. Label these mountains by letter:
   a. Pikes Peak   d. Longs Peak
   b. Wheeler Peak   e. Grand Teton Mountain
   c. Gannett Peak   f. Mt. Elbert
5. Label these cities: Las Vegas, Reno, Idaho Falls, Billings, Great Falls, Butte, Boulder, Colorado Springs, Pueblo, Provo, Ogden, Casper, Laramie, and Pocatello.

Complete the following statements with distances, directions, and features.

6. Boise is about _____ km/mi. _____ of Helena.

7. To go from Colorado Springs to Salt Lake City you would go mostly _____ and would cross the _____ Mountains, the _____ River, the _____ River, and the _____ Range.

8. The Wind River Range lies _____ of the Big Horn Mountains.

9. The _____ Range lies on the Montana–Idaho border.

10. Cheyenne is about _____ km/mi. _____ of Denver.

11. Flying from Carson City to Salt Lake City, a plane would cross the _____ and pass north of _____ Peak.

12. East of the Rocky Mountains lie the _____.

13. _____, the capital of Colorado, is known as the "mile-high city."

14. The _____ Lake is found in Utah.

15. The _____ River flows west through southern Idaho.

16. Carson City (39°N, 120°W) is the capital of _____.

17. The source of the _____ River, which flows through the midwest, is in Montana.

18. The highest peaks in the _____ Mountains are in Colorado.

19. Old Faithful, located in Yellowstone National Park, is in the state of_____.

20. The _____ separates eastward and westward flowing waters.

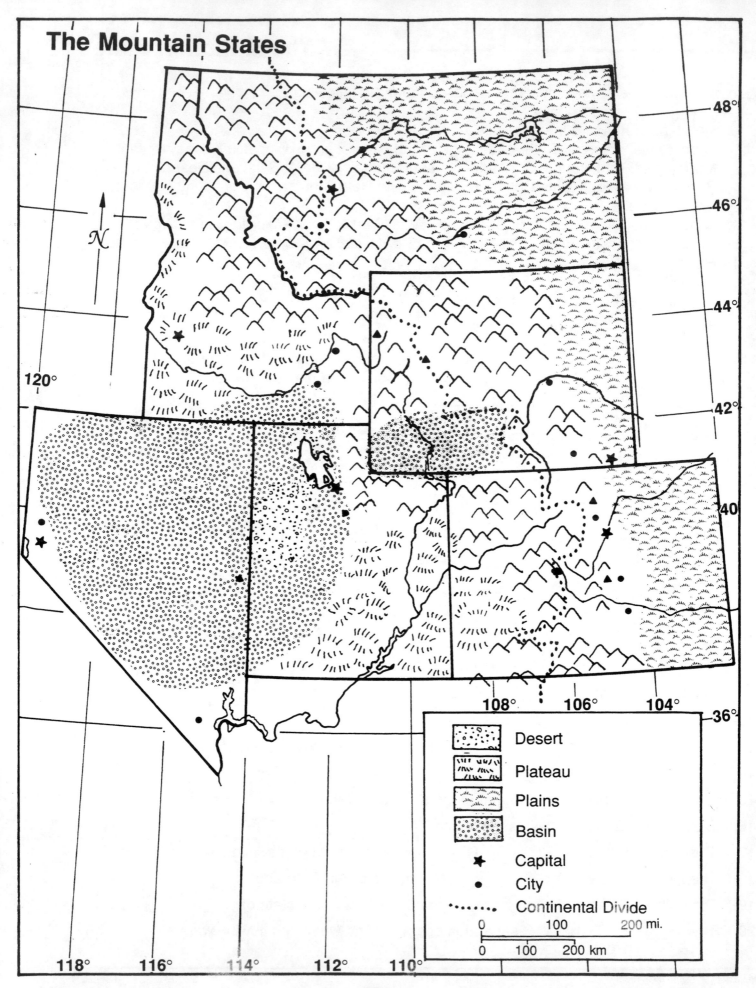

The Mountain States

N

48°

46°

44°

42°

120°

40°

108°   106°   104°

36°

118°   116°   114°   112°   110°

	Desert
	Plateau
	Plains
	Basin
★	Capital
●	City
⋯⋯	Continental Divide

0   100   200 mi.

0   100   200 km

© Milliken Publishing Company

15a

The Pacific States

Use previous maps or additional references to label the following.

1. Label the states and their capitals.
2. Label these features: Mojave Desert, Cascade Range, Coast Ranges, Sierra Nevada, Brooks Range, Alaska Range, Columbia Plateau, Central Valley, Bering Strait, Aleutian Islands, Point Barrow, Death Valley, Lake Tahoe, and Blue Mountains.
3. Label these bodies of water: *Columbia River, Snake River, Yukon River, Colorado River, Pacific Ocean, Arctic Ocean, Gulf of Alaska, Beaufort Sea, Puget Sound, Willamette River, Sacramento River, San Joaquin River,* and *Bering Sea.*
4. Label these mountains by letter:
   a. Mt. McKinley (Denali)   d. Mauna Kea   g. Mt. St. Elias
   b. Mauna Loa   e. Mt. Whitney   h. Mt. Shasta
   c. Mt. St. Helens   f. Mt. Rainier   i. Mt. Hood
5. Label these cities: Los Angeles, San Diego, San Francisco, San Jose, Bakersfield, Long Beach, Eugene, Portland, Tacoma, Seattle, Spokane, Anchorage, Fairbanks, and Hilo.

Across:
2. _____ has the smallest population, but is larger in area than any other state.
3. The only state that is not part of the continent of North America is _____.
6. _____ and sequoia forests cover large areas of land in the Pacific states.
8. At 34°N, 118°W, _____ is the largest city in the Pacific region.
9. Seattle, Washington is on the _____ Sound.
10. The _____ Desert can be found in California.

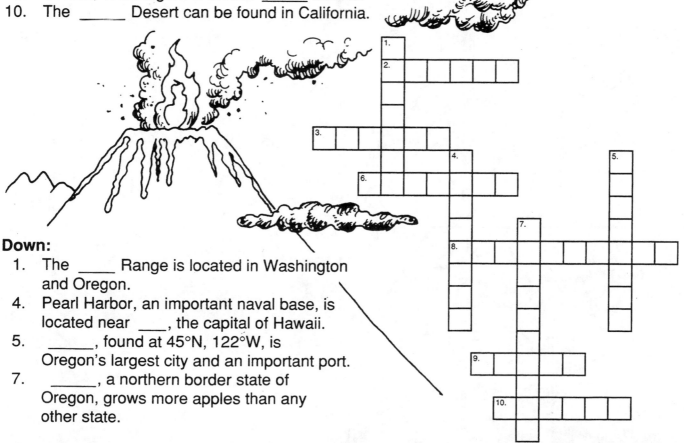

Down:
1. The _____ Range is located in Washington and Oregon.
4. Pearl Harbor, an important naval base, is located near ___, the capital of Hawaii.
5. _____, found at 45°N, 122°W, is Oregon's largest city and an important port.
7. _____, a northern border state of Oregon, grows more apples than any other state.

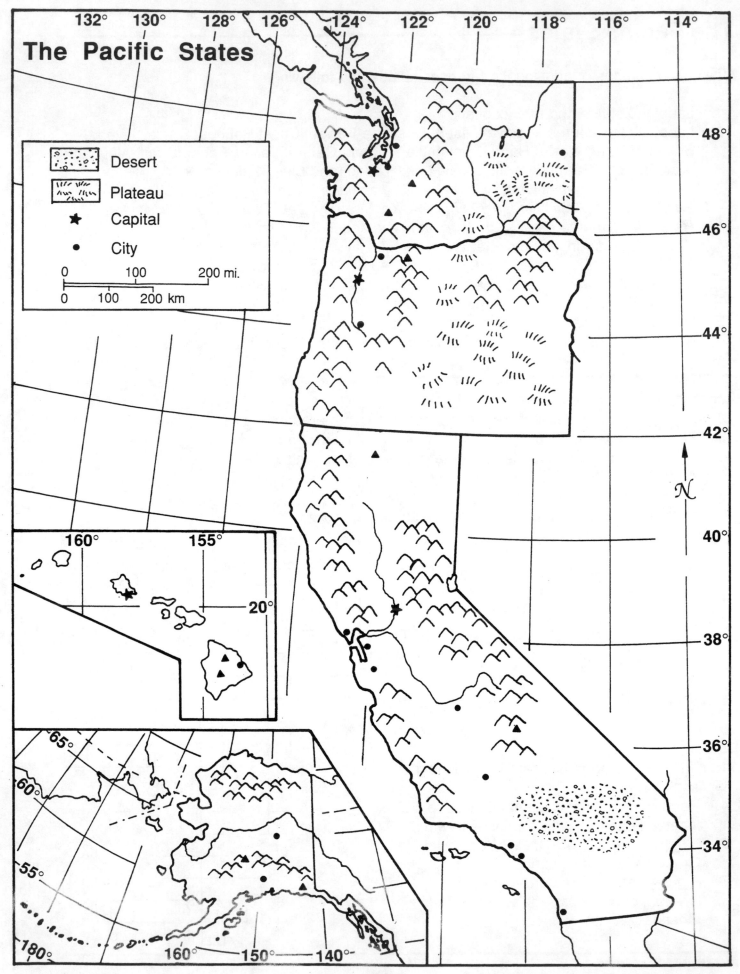

The Pacific States

Desert

Plateau

★ Capital

● City

132° 130° 128° 126° 124° 122° 120° 118° 116° 114°

48°
46°
44°
42°
40°
38°
36°
34°

N

160° 155° 20°

65° 60° 55° 180° 160° 150° 140°